Count Your Way through

Mexico

by Jim Haskins

illustrations by Helen Byers

Carolrhoda Books, Inc./Minneapolis

To Michael and Marcus

Text copyright © 1989 by Jim Haskins
Illustrations copyright © 1989 by Carolrhoda Books, Inc.

This book is available in two editions:
Library binding by Carolrhoda Books, Inc.
Soft cover by First Avenue Editions
c/o The Lerner Group
241 First Avenue North
Minneapolis, Minnesota 55401

LIBRARY OF CONGRESS CATALOGING-IN-PUBLICATION DATA

Haskins, James, 1941-
    Count your way through Mexico / by Jim Haskins ; illustrations
by Helen Byers.
        p. cm.
    Summary: Presents the numbers one to ten in Spanish, using each
number to introduce concepts about Mexico and its culture.
    ISBN 0-87614-349-4 (lib. bdg.)
    ISBN 0-87614-517-9 (pbk.)
    1. Mexico — Civilization — Juvenile literature. 2. Counting —
Juvenile literature. [1. Mexico. 2. Counting.] I. Byers, Helen, ill.
II. Title.
F1210.H35 1989
972 — dc19   88-25899
                                                               CIP
                                                                AC

Manufactured in the United States of America

    6   7   8   9   10   P/SP   99   98   97   96   95   94

Introductory Note

Spanish has been Mexico's official language for more than four centuries. But the original people of Mexico were Indians, and there are about 50 Indian languages and dialects still in use. There are some Indians in Mexico who still do not speak Spanish.

Because Spanish was adopted in Mexico by Indian peoples who already had their own languages, the variety of Spanish spoken by Mexicans has a special lilt. It's called *el canto Mexicano* (el KAHN-to me-hee-KAHN-o), which means "the Mexican song."

Written Spanish uses accents, or marks, above some letters to show which parts of words should be pronounced most strongly. There are no accents in the Spanish numbers one through ten.

PACIFIC

OCEAN

GULF OF
MEXICO

1 uno (OO-no)

Mexico is **one** country in North America. It shares its longest border with the United States. Because its culture is so different from that of other North American countries, Mexico is sometimes called part of Mesoamerica (Middle America, between North and South America). Yet, it was in Mexico that the first great North American center of civilization developed.

Some ideas and customs of Mexican culture spread north, into what is now the United States, and from there, with the Iroquois Indians, into what is now Canada. An example is the cultivation of maize, or corn.

2 dos (doce)

The recent history of Mexico is the story of the struggle of **two** peoples, the native Indians and the Spanish, to live together. In the early 1500s, a band of strange men arrived by sea in what the Aztec Indians called "houses that float." They were the Spanish *Conquistadores* (kone-kees-ta-DOR-es), or conquerors. Within two years, they had defeated the Aztecs and established the colony of New Spain.

Spain ruled the land for three centuries, until Mexico won its political independence in 1821, after 11 years of painful struggle. By that time, the culture of many Mexicans was more Spanish than Indian. Today, most of the Mexican people are of mixed blood and take a special pride in their Indian and Spanish heritage.

3 tres (trace)

The Day of the **Three** Kings, or Wisemen, on January 6 is one of the most important holidays in Mexico. In Spanish, it is called *el Día de los Reyes* (el DEE-ah day los RAY'es). It celebrates the Christian event of Epiphany, when the three kings, or Magi, visited the Christ child in the manger. The Spaniards brought Roman Catholicism to Mexico, and today most Mexicans are Catholics.

On January 6 each year, many towns in Mexico have a parade. Men wearing huge papier-mâché masks representing the three kings are its main attraction. Traditionally, this is the day on which children receive Christmas presents. As on just about every other Mexican holiday, many people set off firecrackers, which were introduced to Mexico by the Spanish.

4 cuatro (KWA-tro)

There are **four** sides to a pyramid. Mexico has many ancient pyramids, which were built by the Aztecs, Mayans and Totonacs, and even earlier Indian civilizations. One of the largest is the Pyramid of the Sun at Teotihuacán (tay-o-tee-wah-KAHN). It was built by one of the earliest Indian tribes, and it is 210 feet high.

Today, many of these ancient structures are only ruins. Before the Spanish came, warring tribes of Indians knocked down each others' pyramids and temples. Later, the *Conquistadores* destroyed many of the remaining buildings. There are hundreds of these ancient ruins in Mexico.

5 cinco (SING-ko)

Five men take part in the *volador* (vo-la-DOR), the flying pole dance. One is a musician, and the other four are *voladores* (vo-la-DOR-es), or fliers. This exciting dance dates back to the days before the Aztecs.

A small, turning platform is put on top of a pole about 100 feet high. All five men climb up a ladder to the top. The musician plays and dances. The *voladores* are dressed as birds or are wearing feather crests. Each of these four men ties one end of a rope around his waist and leaps out into space. Then the musician lies down on top of the platform. Each flier swoops around the pole 13 times. With each swoop, more rope is unwound from the top of the pole until the *voladores* are near the ground.

While its exact meaning has been lost, we know that the *volador* celebrates an ancient Totonac Indian idea of time. The Totonacs measured a century as 52 years. Four men times 13 swoops around the pole equals 52.

6 seis (sace)

Los Niños Héroes (los NEEN-yos AIR-o-es) are the **six** boy heroes
of Mexico's war with the United States in 1846-48. In that war, the
United States tried to take over Mexico. The six boys were cadets
at the military academy in Chapultepec Castle, near Mexico City.
As the U.S. army invaded, the cadets made a desperate attempt to
defend the castle and the school, shouting *"¡Viva México! ¡Viva el
Colegio Militar!"* (VEE-vah MEH-hee-co! VEE-vah el co-LEH-hee-o
mee-lee-TAR!), which means "Long live Mexico! Long live the
Military School!"

They were killed in the battle, which the U.S. forces won. The
monument to the young heroes is a national shrine. Their names were
Juan de la Barrera, Francisco Marquez, Fernando Montes de Oca,
Agustín Melgar, Vicente Súarez, and Juan Escutia.

7 siete (see-EH-tay)

Seven arts and crafts for which Mexico is famous are: pottery, silver and gold work, basketry, leather work, weaving, woodwork, and glass blowing.

Many Mexicans earn their livings by making craft items for export and to sell to the millions of tourists who visit Mexico each year.

8 ocho (O-cho)

Eight foods given to the world by Mexico are corn, chocolate, tomatoes, vanilla, pumpkins, avocados, chilis, and coconuts. In fact, the words *chocolate* and *tomato* come to us from the Aztec language.

Of these foods, corn is the greatest contribution to the world, for from corn we get not only corn on the cob, but also cornmeal and corn oil. Corn is the basic food of the Mexican diet. Tortillas (thin cornmeal pancakes) are served with most meals, like bread or rolls in the United States. Tacos, enchiladas, tamales, quesadillas, chalupas, gorditas, flautas, and tostadas all use tortillas, topped or filled with meat, cheese, and vegetables.

9 nueve (noo-EH-vay)

A complete bullfight will have **nine** contestants: six bulls and three men to fight them. Each bullfighter will face two bulls, one at a time. The men are called *matadores* (mah-tah-DOR-es), or killers of the bulls. The bulls are *toros bravos* (TO-ros BRA-vos), or brave bulls, and they are especially bred for fighting. These fighting bulls are huge and powerful, and they are very dangerous opponents.

Bullfighting is one of the most popular spectator sports in Mexico, just as it is in Spain. It was introduced to Mexico by the Spanish.

10 diez (dee-ES)

Ten creatures native to Mexico include five mammals, three reptiles, and two birds. The chihuahua is the world's smallest dog. The prairie dog isn't a dog at all, but a rodent that burrows into the ground for shelter. The burro doesn't burrow; it is a small donkey. The jaguar is one of the rarest big cats in the animal kingdom. The opossum is one of the strangest animals, because it hangs from its tail and sleeps upside down.

The iguana is a big, but harmless, lizard. The coral snake is small and poisonous. And the desert tortoise is as slow-moving as its non-desert relatives.

Both the parrot and the quetzal bird have brightly colored feathers. The quetzal was sacred to the Aztecs, who used its tail feathers in headdresses for their priests and kings.

Pronunciation Guide

1 / **uno** / OO-no

2 / **dos** / doce

3 / **tres** / trace

4 / **cuatro** / KWA-tro

5 / **cinco** / SING-ko

6 / **seis** / sace

7 / **siete** / see-EH-tay

8 / **ocho** / O-cho

9 / **nueve** / noo-EH-vay

10 / **diez** / dee-ES